COSTUMES and MAKEUP

rosen publishing's
rosen
central®
New York

Doretta Lau

In memory of Rosita Engstrand

Published in 2010 by The Rosen Publishing Group, Inc.
29 East 21st Street, New York, NY 10010

Library of Congress Cataloging-in-Publication Data

Lau, Doretta.
Costumes and makeup / Doretta Lau.
  p. cm.—(High school musicals)
Includes bibliographical references and index.
ISBN-13: 978-1-4358-5258-7 (library binding)
ISBN-13: 978-1-4358-5530-4 (pbk)
ISBN-13: 978-1-4358-5531-1 (6 pack)
1. Musicals—Production and direction. 2. Costume. I. Title.
MT955.L376 2009
792.602'6—dc22

2008046076

6345

Manufactured in Malaysia

Contents

INTRODUCTION

Costumes and makeup can transform any actor in a musical from young to old, plain to glamorous. A hat, a hairstyle, and carefully planned makeup are just a few details that go into creating a complete look for every character in a production, no matter how big or small the role. A good costume gives the audience a lot of information about a character's age, social status, and personality. As well, hair and makeup highlight when and where the musical is set, telling a story without a single line of dialogue or note of music.

For a high school musical, the right costume and expertly applied makeup can make even the smallest production take on a professional aura. A single signature piece (a special costume item that helps define a character), like the mask the Phantom wears in *The Phantom of the Opera*, can help cast a spell on the audience

Lopez High students from Brownsville, Texas, don feathers, masks, and formal clothing for a performance of Andrew Lloyd Webber's *The Phantom of the Opera*.

and create the necessary magic for a good show. Imagination and creativity, rather than a large budget, are the keys to successful costume and makeup design.

Many musical theater professionals got their start in high school. Costumer Blake Anderson put on his first play in his family's garage when he was five years old. While attending Kaneland High School in Illinois, Anderson acted in productions by Playmakers, Inc. and Pheasant Run Resort and Spa Hotel. His love of the stage prompted him to study theater at Northern Illinois University and apprentice at the Little Theatre on the Square in Downstate Sullivan.

As an actor, Anderson appeared in *Jesus Christ Superstar* and *Hair*. After playing numerous roles in *Hair*, he managed, directed, and choreographed a production that toured nationally. His career took him from Chicago to New York and Los Angeles. Eventually, he settled back in Illinois and discovered his true passion: costume making and design. He founded a company called Stage Rags and, over the course of thirteen years, proceeded to perfect his design and costuming craft for community theater and high schools. For a production of *Hello, Dolly!*, Anderson killed a rooster on his family's farm and, with the assistance of a taxidermist (a person who prepares, stuffs, and mounts animal skins), used the feathers to create a hat for the musical's title character. Every detail in a costume was important to him, even ones that the audience would never see, like suit pockets and coat linings.

Throughout his life, Anderson maintained a love for musical theater. He believed that everyone was entitled to a good theater experience without having to spend a great deal of money. This is likely the reason he was so dedicated to making costumes for community theaters and high schools. People of all ages who lived in his area were able to enjoy professional costuming for all sorts of productions, no matter how grand or simple.

In the twilight of his career, Anderson was able to continue making costumes and had the opportunity to star in *Oliver!* as Fagan. After he sold his company, he continued to design and make costumes for high school productions, parties, and performers like singer Kenny Rogers. When Anderson died in 2008 at the age of sixty-one, his contribution to musical theater had affected a great many people and dazzled countless audiences.

As you can see, every role in a musical theater production is important to the overall result. Costumes and makeup are as necessary as actors and music to any successful show. You don't need to know how to sing and dance to take part in the creative process.

A Team Effort

Are you thinking about staging a musical at your school? The first thing to remember is that musical theater is a collaborative effort, meaning that it takes a team of people to make it happen. In addition to the actors and director, there are numerous backstage roles ranging from the technical to the creative. When everyone works together and everything goes smoothly, the audience is sure to be dazzled by the performance and the look of the show.

Think about a musical performance that you enjoyed. What did the costumes look like? Was there anything about the makeup that was special? Were the hairstyles complicated? Write down what you liked, and then write down what you thought could have been done better. You can apply these ideas to your own musical theater production. This attention to detail is needed to make the costumes and makeup perfect for your school musical.

It requires a team of people with different interests, skills, and talents to successfully create the costumes, hair, and makeup for a musical.

The Creative Team

The people who are in charge of costumes and makeup for a musical are part of the creative team. The creative team in a professional production may include the following: producer,

director, composer, lyricist, librettist, musical director, choreographer, set designer, costume designer, lighting designer, sound designer, accent coach, skills coach, fight director, assistant director, assistant musical director, band, singing captain, dance captain, and the cast. There are also "dressers" who help the actors change quickly between scenes. The costume designer oversees the wardrobe supervisor, head of wigs, and head makeup artist. In turn, the wardrobe supervisor oversees the cutters, makers, dressers, and wardrobe maintenance; the head of wigs oversees the wig assistants; and the head makeup artist oversees the makeup assistants. In smaller productions, many of these roles can be combined or eliminated. For instance, your production may have no need for cutters and makers. The key is to decide, with the help of the director and producer, how many people you need to make the creative team run smoothly and efficiently.

The Costume Designer

The head of the creative team is called the costume designer. Depending on the number of people who want to volunteer for the musical, the costume designer can supervise up to three department heads: wardrobe supervisor, head of wigs, and head makeup artist. If you don't plan on using wigs for your production, there can be a volunteer who is the head hairstylist.

The costume designer reports to the director and works with him or her to decide how many costumes are needed for the show. Every actor and dancer in the show needs to be outfitted. Once this number has been determined, the costume designer consults with the set designer to decide on a color palette for the fabrics and makeup to ensure that the costumes and the set work together visually. Costumes and makeup tell a story and add to the overall narrative. All decisions regarding the visual elements of the show must be made before the costume designer begins to assemble the wardrobe for each character, or the production will risk unnecessary work and cost.

With color scheme and general idea of the set in mind and after some research, the costume designer draws a full set of costume sketches for each character in the show. The drawings should include as much detail as possible, so that everyone in the production can refer back to the drawings for guidance. The completed set of sketches will allow the costume designer to work with the wardrobe supervisor to make, borrow, buy, or rent the

The key to staging a great musical is for the costume designer, director, wardrobe supervisor, head makeup artist, and head hairstylist to effectively communicate with one another.

necessary items for each actor. While sourcing all the necessary materials for the costumes, the costume designer will check in with the production manager to ensure that the costs are within budget. The costume designer is responsible for overseeing costume rentals and loans for any item that isn't custom made for the production and ensuring that everything is returned in excellent condition.

Once a fair number of costumes and items have been made, bought, borrowed, or rented, the costume designer and wardrobe supervisor work together to make sure that the costumes match the original concept of the drawings. If adjustments must be made, the costume designer has to keep in mind the look of the set, the budget, and how the costumes will affect a character's presentation to the audience.

When the costumes are ready, the costume designer oversees the fittings. The actors will try on the costumes and the costume designer will oversee any necessary alterations. The final costumes need to be ready for the dress rehearsal, where the costume designer will watch the entire production to make sure that everything goes according to plan and to address any costuming issues before the show opens.

Wardrobe Supervisor

The wardrobe supervisor's job is to help the costume designer with any costuming issues and to oversee the finished and borrowed or rented costumes. If the musical has many actors, scene changes, and seasons, there could be more than a hundred costumes to look after! This is a big job and requires a very organized, careful, and responsible person.

The costume designer may ask the wardrobe supervisor to source the right fabric for a costume or to ask the cast, friends, and parents for specific items like hats, shoes, and dresses.

Though the wardrobe supervisor will be doing a lot of work before the show opens, the nights of the show will be the most demanding. The wardrobe supervisor will need to make sure that the actors know where their costumes are and the order in which they need to wear them. Any missing item or slow wardrobe change can affect the production.

Head Makeup Artist

The head makeup artist's job is to help the costume designer decide on the right makeup for each actor. Many of the actors may require

Recruiting Your Creative Team

Recruiting students to help join the creative team may take some time and effort, but anyone at your school who loves clothing, makeup, or styling hair can contribute a lot. Every shoelace, fake eyelash, and ponytail adds to the overall visual effect of the production, so the talents of many are needed to make the production a success. Put up signs or posters around the school. Look around for students who can draw, wear interesting clothing, or simply seem to have an artistic eye. Any student with the time and dedication can learn a lot and contribute to the creative team and musical production. You will be amazed at how many people will want to sign up!

some help to look older in order to be believable in the roles they are playing. Some actors may need to look younger onstage.

If the actors are skilled at doing their own makeup, the head makeup artist will work with the costume designer on developing a look, and the actors can apply their makeup according to the preplanned look.

Actors Michael Ball (*left*) and Leanne Jones wear elaborate wigs and psychedelic print, feather-trimmed dresses with 1960s silhouettes for a London, England, production of *Hairspray*.

Head of Wigs or Head Hairstylist

Many professional theater productions use wigs. You may or may not have access to wigs for your high school musical. More than likely, you will only have access to the hair your actors already have. The head hairstylist will work with the costume designer to

determine how each actor's hair should look. Some costume changes may also require a quick hair change. It is up to the head hairstylist to come up with a plan of action for all hair needs. This may require a number of extra people backstage to help out during dress rehearsal and the run of the show, so it is best to teach actors how to prepare their own hair.

These four positions are the most important for the costume and makeup departments. Other jobs can be added, depending on the number of volunteers who want to help with the production. Every freshman, sophomore, junior, and senior interested in lending a hand should have a role and important responsibilities. But no matter what each person's title may be, in the end the most important thing is for everyone to work together to follow the director's vision. Practice, collaboration, communication, and cooperation are key to staging a successful show.

2
CHAPTER

Planning Makes Perfect!

You've probably heard people tell you that practice makes perfect. In the case of creating the costume and makeup look for your production, planning makes perfect. You may want to start a notebook for your production. You can write down all of your ideas and make lists of things that need to be done in order to stage a great show. The other important thing to remember to do is to communicate with the other members of the creative team. Every decision you make needs to fit within the director's vision for the production.

If you think of each thing that needs to be done as a step toward the final product, it will make accomplishing each task more manageable and less stressful. It is only possible to take one step at a time when completing your journey. And if you feel overwhelmed, don't be afraid to ask for help. That is what your team is for.

Make lists and timelines for every single thing that needs to be acquired or done before the dress rehearsal. No item is too small to put on a list!

Counting Your Pennies

Before you start imagining a lavish production, the first thing you must do is go over the budget with the producer or teacher in charge. A tip to remember: a musical generally costs five to eight times more to stage than a play, mostly due to a larger cast. Purchase costs to consider include clothes, hats, shoes, accessories, fabric, and decorations. Rental costs may include uniforms and period costumes. In professional productions, there are labor costs for making costumes. But for a high school production, it is best to find volunteers willing to donate their time and expertise.

The amount of money set aside for costumes and makeup will influence what you can buy and how you go about acquiring items that you need for the production. Don't think of the budget as a limitation—think of it as an incentive to use your creativity and imagination to solve problems. Come up with ideas that fit within your budget. If you do not believe that the money allotted for costumes and makeup is enough, you can hold fund-raisers and ask local organizations to donate necessary items in exchange for advertisement in the show program.

Making a Timeline

Above all else, the costumes must be ready in time for the dress rehearsal. This is the main goal of the costume designer and everyone who is working on making and sourcing costumes. A missing costume is like a missing instrument in the orchestra the night of a show—the audience will know that something is wrong. Therefore, it is extremely important to make a timeline and follow it. That way, everything will be in place before the show opens.

Your Timeline

During rehearsals, the timeline may be set up in the following way:

- **First rehearsal** The costume designer attends rehearsal and takes actor measurements. The heads of makeup and hair also attend to meet the actors.
- **Five to six weeks prior to opening night** The search for costumes, fabrics, shoes, makeup, and hair accessories begins.
- **Three to four weeks prior to opening night** The costume designer does preliminary fittings of costumes and sourced items. At this time, the heads of makeup and hair can test their designs and ideas on actors.
- **Two weeks prior to opening night** Final touches on costumes and final fittings should be done.
- **Six to seven days prior to opening night** Costumes should be moved to the dressing areas and stored in an organized fashion in order to keep everything clean and unwrinkled. Any final fittings should take place during this time.
- **Run-through and technical rehearsal** Costume designer, wardrobe supervisor, makeup, and hair should attend run-through and technical rehearsal to check for any possible issues that might come up. Makeup should be checked under stage lighting. Costumes should maneuver easily onstage.
- **Dress rehearsal** Costume designer and makeup artists should check for any necessary final changes.
- **Final rehearsal** All costumes and makeup should remain the same from this point forward, barring any last-minute emergencies.

Prior to the rehearsals, the creative team will need to meet in order to discuss the vision for the look of the show. During this time, the costume designer will begin research and make drawings of every costume to be used. As well, the team will work together to stay within budget and look for fabric stores, thrift shops, and costume rental companies.

Reading the Libretto

The costume designer must read over the libretto— the full script containing both lyrics and dialogue— carefully during the prerehearsal period to get a sense of how to dress the actors. When reading, he or she should look for things like time period, setting, season, and number of characters that appear during the course of the production. It is very important to accurately count the number of actors and dancers who will be onstage, whether they have speaking parts or not. Every actor and dancer, no matter how

Julie Andrews is shown here in 1956 as Eliza Doolittle in *My Fair Lady*. Notice how her costume looks old and her face slightly dirty.

small the part, must have costumes for every single scene in which they appear.

Some actors may require a number of costume changes, which can become expensive if the costumes are not properly planned. Take note of the major priorities and work from there. For instance, if the star of the show undergoes a transformation, like Eliza

The library is a great resource for researching the specific costumes, makeup, and hair needed for a musical production set during a certain time period.

Doolittle in *My Fair Lady*, her wardrobe must look noticeably different as the musical progresses. If a minor character does not go through any major changes during the course of the show, it is possible to mix and match elements of the costume from scene to scene, or to simply add accessories to alter a look slightly.

Once the costume designer has read over the libretto, he or she should consult with the director and choreographer to finalize how many costumes will be required for each actor.

Research

The costume designer and the set designer must discuss the palette— the colors—that will be used in both the costumes and the set. All the elements of the production should come together to present a strong visual story. There is no sense in acquiring costumes that clash with or blend into the set. When the creative team has determined the palette, as well as the time period, setting, and season that the production takes place, it is time to start researching.

There are a few things to keep in mind when you are researching. Get a sense of the general shape and outline of the clothes worn in the time period the musical is set. Ask yourself why the clothes are constructed this way. Does it have to do with the current events of the time? How does the shape of the clothing relate to the class of person who might wear the clothes? Take a close look at how clothes are constructed and note what kind of fabric is popular for the clothing of the time period. Examine accessories, hairstyles, makeup, and other details in paintings and photographs.

If the production your school is doing has been staged before, look for photos of a staged performance, or see if it is available on DVD. You don't have to follow what the costume designer did for the previous production—it's just an opportunity to get some ideas and direction. Watch films from the period the musical is set in to get a sense of the costumes. Go to a costume museum, if there is one available in your area, to see costumes in person. Also have a look at photos, drawings, and paintings of people from the time period the musical is set in. All these resources can influence the look of your production.

Costume Drawings

After a good amount of research is done, the costume designer can draw a full set of costumes for each character. The number of costumes should be decided upon by the director before starting on this large project. These drawings will serve as a guide for all the people helping make or find each item needed. It is therefore very important to be as detailed as possible when preparing the costume drawings.

For period costumes, pay careful attention to details like accessories and trim. Here, a woman in 1899 is wearing a lace-trimmed dress and a hat, and she is carrying a parasol.

Color

When discussing the palette of the production with the set designer, it is helpful to understand color. There are three primary colors: red, yellow, and blue. Every color on the wheel in the picture is made from a combination of the primary colors. The mixture of the primary colors results in secondary colors: orange, green, and purple. Colors opposite each other on the wheel are complementary. When complementary colors are mixed together, the resulting color is grey. An important aspect to remember about color is that there are hot shades and cool shades, which has to do with the psychological reaction we have with these colors. Red and orange are warm, while blue and green are cool. This may come in handy when interpreting a costume for a specific leading character. Perhaps the character begins the musical acting rather aloof and warms up as the story progresses. Finally, very brightly colored clothing was not possible until after 1910, when chemical dyes were manufactured and used on fabrics. All period costumes prior to 1910 should have fabrics that look like they were treated with natural dyes.

The drawings do not have to be works of art. They need to clearly communicate the basic idea about the costumes: shape, color, and design. The figures in the drawings should reflect real proportions because the costuming team must be able to make or find costumes that reflect the ideas and fit the actors. As well, it is incredibly important for the costumes to allow actors to run, dance, and fight with as much ease as possible. Stiletto heels and heavy garments should be avoided in physically demanding scenes.

Each drawing should show the front view. If the costume is slightly more complicated, it should also show a side or three-quarter view to give a sense of any complicated details. Sketch a line down the middle of the body to help with positioning pockets, buttons, and lapels.

One of the quickest ways to prepare the numerous drawings needed for each costume is to make a stencil of a figure and use it over and over again. To do this, draw a figure on a piece of thick paper or poster board and cut it out.

If drawing is too difficult, substitute it with photographs, clippings from magazines, and photocopies from fashion books to give a sense of what is needed. Collages made of fabrics and magazine clippings can also communicate costuming ideas. Save any pictures of hairstyles for the hairstylist.

Once the drawings are complete, the director must approve each costume before the costume designer can begin making and searching for each shirt, skirt, coat, and pair of trousers.

Drawing Basic Proportions

Study a full-length picture of a fashion model. Take note of the head, torso, arms, and legs. Then, think of the human figure as a series of shapes: cones, cylinders, and spheres. Visualize the head as a sphere, and the neck as a cylinder. The torso is two inverted cones.

The costume designer must prepare a set of costume drawings for each character. These drawings serve as a guide for sourcing the necessary wardrobe items.

The arms and legs are cylinders. Costumes fit onto a figure in the same way—sleeves and pant legs are cylinders, while skirts are cone-like.

The head of a figure should fit seven times into the body. Arms should reach mid-thigh when extended down. Eyes are two-thirds up the face, while the tops of the ears are level with the eyes. The nose should be within the lower half of the head and the mouth in the bottom third.

Sew, Shop, Rent, and Borrow: Making and Acquiring the Costumes

As soon as casting is complete, it's time to take measurements for each actor. The first rehearsal is the perfect opportunity to complete this task. Consult with the director to formulate an efficient plan for measuring each actor. Rehearsals can be long and tiring; it is important to prevent cast members from having too much unnecessary downtime. Don't forget to measure the understudies, if there are any, in addition to the actors for last-minute alterations and costuming should an emergency situation arise.

Make an actor measurements chart, like the one on page 30.

Make one copy of this chart for each actor and understudy in the production. Do not let actors fill in this information on their own unless it is impossible to take measurements in person. The costume designer must use a measuring tape and record each measurement when possible. Every inch and foot must be exact to ensure that each item fits correctly. Head measurements are essential to finding hats and wigs that fit. The outside leg to ground measurement is

Actor Measurement Chart

Name:

Contact information:

Ususal dress/shirt/pants size:

Height:

Chest/bust:

Waist:

Hips:

Nape to waist [back]:

Nape to waist [front]:

Across back:

Across front:

Across shoulders:

Shoulders:

Armhole:

Underarm to waist:

Shoulder-elbow-wrist [bent]:

Inside arm [straight]:

Neck:

Inside leg:

Outside leg [to knee]:

Outside leg [to ground]:

Shoe size:

Circumference of head:

Wrist:

Forearm:

Elbow:

Pierced ears?:

Under knee:

Above knee:

Thigh:

Shown above is a sample actor measurement chart. The costume designer will take measurements of each actor and record the information on a chart like this one. Each actor and understudy will get a copy of this chart.

key to making skirts and dresses the right length. Correct arm measurements prevent jackets from looking like they were borrowed from shorter or taller people.

When the measurement chart is complete, consult with the actor to see if he or she owns any of the items of clothing needed for his or her character. This will help keep the production within budget and make the task of costuming each actor easier. You can make a copy of the set of costume drawings for each actor to take home so

A properly fitted costume goes a long way in making an outfit, and the actor wearing the outfit, more believable to the audience.

that he or she will be able to remember what to look for. The actor's personal wardrobe, storage closets, and attic may end up being valuable costuming resources. After the first rehearsal, e-mail all the actors with a reminder that everyone should check their closets and ask their parents for help. Actors should bring costume items to rehearsal the following week. The costume designer can then examine all items to ensure that everything fits with the director's vision and make a list of items still needed.

The first rehearsal is also a good time to inquire whether or not an actor's mom or dad may want to volunteer to sew costumes or if any cast members know of costuming resources. Again, communication is key to getting the job done well.

Costume Sourcing

The options for sourcing costumes vary depending on the time period in which the musical is set. For modern musicals like *Legally Blonde*, it may be possible to attain nearly all the items from cast members, friends, and family. As well, regular boutiques and department stores will likely carry many of the necessary garments and accessories.

For other time periods, thrift stores and costume rental shops may yield a number of the costumes. Remember to take the set of costume drawings along on shopping trips to ensure that no detail gets missed in the process. Make a grid of every actor and the costumes needed for the show. Make a column to record where each costume came from so that it can be returned to the correct rental shop or person when the show is over. This grid will also be handy for the wardrobe supervisor, who will have to check that all the costumes are complete before final rehearsals.

The bright, modern-style costumes worn by Bailey Hanks and her costars set the mood, season, and time period for the musical version of *Legally Blonde*.

Before setting off on a costume sourcing expedition, a little research may cut down on unnecessary trips and frustrating searches. Check the Internet for all local thrift and charity shops. Also make a list of local costume shops and rental companies. Call the thrift stores to find out how large their inventory is and whether or not they may have what you're looking for. This way, it is possible to prioritize which store to visit first.

How to Adapt Old Clothes or Make New Clothes Look Old

Attics and thrift stores are filled with possible costumes. Remember that a garment that looks promising may need only a few small changes to be perfect. A shirt collar can be changed to reflect a specific time period. An alteration in a collar's shape or in fabric can take it from modern to Edwardian. New buttons can make a shirt look more expensive, more fashionable, or from an earlier century. Extra buttons on a shirt or jacket can alter it to look like a period costume. Shoulder pads can be added or removed to change the silhouette of a jacket.

For women's costumes, the alteration of a skirt's hem can change a look drastically, taking it from one decade to the next. Additionally, trimmings like ribbon and lace can transform a plain dress into party finery.

Washing and pressing a garment can sometimes transform it. Simply ironing a collar to form it to a new shape or taking the crease out of a pair of trousers can give it the look of a different time period.

If a costume is brand new and needs to look worn, there are several things that can be done. The actor can begin wearing it during every rehearsal before the show opens. Remember to allow time for the costume to be laundered regularly to prevent makeup stains from setting. Sometimes, having a garment dry-cleaned will give it that desired worn-in look. You can also age fabrics by scuffing them with rough items like bricks or sandpaper. A few well-placed wear marks and the use of spray-on dye can give a costume the desired lived-in feel.

Making the Costumes

Any wardrobe items that can't be found in actors' closets, thrift stores, costume shops, or rental agencies need to be made. The costume designer cannot complete this task alone. There are simply too many costumes that will need attention and alteration.

One school resource that the costume designer should consider is the home economics department. The costume designer and a sewing class could team up to create the costumes as a term project. Access to sewing machines and possible volunteers will be key to getting numerous costumes completed, fitted, and altered in time for the dress rehearsals.

Sourcing Fabric

For costumes made from scratch, one of the most important elements to consider is the fabric. Look at the costume drawings and determine what fabrics may be suitable for each item. Some costumes many require a stiff burlap, while others will call for a delicate chiffon.

Before setting off to shop, be sure to write down the quantity of fabric needed for each costume. Voluminous ball gowns will

The production team and a sewing class at your school can team up to create all the dresses, pants, jackets, skirts, and shirts needed to costume the cast.

require far more material than a tailored uniform. This careful planning will make the visit to the store go more smoothly and avoid fabric shortage or waste.

In addition to fabric stores, investigate other sources for cloth. Go to garage sales and charity shops in search of old bedspreads, curtains, tablecloths, and blankets. Many of these fabrics will have a worn-in look to them, which will be perfect for productions that have rags-to-riches storylines. Another budget-friendly idea is to have a fabric drive at school and ask students to donate any discarded fabric items from their homes to the production.

Fabric Types

- acrylic
- bombazine
- brocade
- burlap
- calico
- canvas
- cashmere
- chiffon
- chintz
- crepe
- crushed velvet
- flannel
- felt
- herringbone
- jersey

- lawn
- moiré
- nylon
- organdy
- organza
- panne velvet
- polyester
- rayon
- satin
- taffeta
- terry cloth
- twill
- velvet
- velvet brocade
- velveteen

Fitting a Costume

The first costume fitting is one of the most important times in the production for the costume designer. As well, it gives the performers an idea of how their costumes can enhance their performances.

The fitting should take place in front of a full-length mirror. The costume designer and wardrobe supervisor should be present. One

A full-length mirror is a necessary tool when fitting a costume. The actor will wear the costume, while the costume designer directs an assistant to pin hems and seams.

person can pin hems and seams, while the other directs the action. The actor must stand up straight for the duration of the fitting to ensure that hem levels and proportions are correct. Use tailor's chalk to mark off any changes to neckline and lapel shapes.

Ask the actor if the costume is too restrictive for dance numbers or regular movements. Adjust accordingly. Make sure that the outfit is taking shape based on the original costume drawings. Any changes made in the early stages of the costume will be done more easily than when the garment is complete.

Padding a Costume

If the libretto calls for a character to be portly and the actor chosen for the part is thin, it is possible to make the actor appear heavier using padding. The best padding material is made of polyester wadding, which is a lightweight and washable material. It is best to avoid using foam rubber because it can be difficult to keep clean.

Use a T-shirt in the actor's normal size as the base for the padding. Place the shirt on a tailor's dummy to ensure that the proportions will be correct. The wadding should go on the stomach, not the chest area.

Cut out circular pieces of the polyester wadding in decreasing sizes. Pin the largest piece to the stomach area first, then pin the next largest piece of wadding on top. The effect should look like a layered target. Repeat until you achieve the desired shape, then glue each layer with latex adhesive. Sew every layer in place with large tacking stitches. Finally, cover the area with fine muslin to hold all the layers in place. Or, cover the entire T-shirt with another T-shirt in the next size up.

Getting the Actors to Look Their Best

Hair and makeup provide the finishing touch to an actor's look. Makeup should enhance, not overpower, the face. Since the 1960s, new lighting technologies have eliminated the need for heavy makeup. Orange-based makeup looks old-fashioned and fake. Therefore, the rule for makeup is: less is more. If makeup is noticeable in the second and third rows, it is too heavy and should be toned down to a look that is more natural. Keep in mind the different skin tones of your actors. Apply makeup in a way that complements the way they look naturally.

The makeup artist should work with the palette that has been decided upon by the costume designer and set designer. Determine if the makeup needs to change from act to act for each individual actor. Perhaps a character's health declines throughout the musical. Or, the narrative happens over a

An actor can learn how to do his or her own makeup, which can be applied with fingers and hands. Brushes are useful for fine touches and precise lines.

period of ten or twenty years. What makeup is necessary? Does the actor require aging makeup or application of facial hair?

Tools of the Trade

A basic makeup kit includes cotton balls, tissue, a clean towel, sponges, brushes, a mirror, cake makeup, creme makeup, greasepaint, makeup pencils, mascara, eye shadow, face powders, hair whiteners, makeup removers, and adhesives.

Consult with the cast to see if they have their own personal makeup kits that they can bring in for dress rehearsal and for the

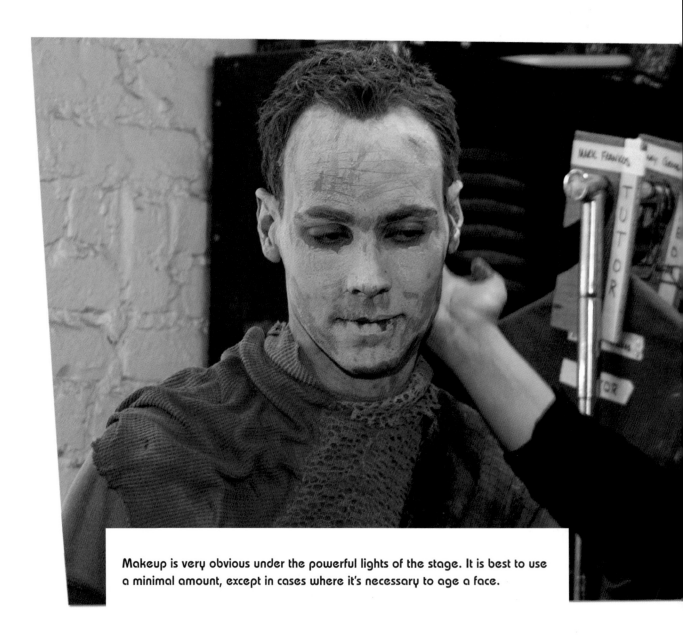

Makeup is very obvious under the powerful lights of the stage. It is best to use a minimal amount, except in cases where it's necessary to age a face.

run of the show. If some actors can be taught how to apply their own makeup, it will make preshow preparations each evening less complicated and stressful. Parents of some of the actors might want to lend a hand as well. Minor characters could even apply their makeup at home beforehand.

Applying Makeup

Makeup application is a three-step process. First, foundation is applied to the face. For all three types of foundation, be sure to cover the entire face, from the hairline down to the neck. Cake makeup should be stroked onto the skin with a damp sponge until the face is covered with a thin film of paint. There is no need for powder. Creme makeup is applied thinly on the face with fingers, a brush, or a sponge, and finished with a powder.

If using the stick or tube form of greasepaint as the foundation, ensure that the face is clean before applying with the fingers. When using the hard greasepaint sticks, first apply cold cream to the face. Then, mix the greasepaint colors in the palm to achieve the desired color and to avoid random blobs of makeup appearing on the face. Rub palms together and wipe a thin layer of grease-paint on the face using smooth strokes. It is important to ensure that the foundation is spread on thinly to allow for highlighting and shadowing effects to be applied on top in the next step. Greasepaint should be fixed with a powder.

The second step is modeling the face with highlights and shadows. Think of this step as emphasizing light and shade on the face. Under a spotlight, the brightest parts of the face are the top of the nose, the cheekbones, and the forehead. Light hitting the soft fold of flesh under the eyes causes wrinkles and black circles to be prominent, which can be addressed with a concealing makeup. Highlighting areas of emphasis and shading the surrounding area is the key to stage makeup. Each feature on the face can be made narrower or more prominent through highlighting and shading.

Use a brush to apply cake or creme makeup over foundation. Apply the darkest tone first. Clean the brush before blending the shadows into the foundation. Then, add highlights beside the dark areas to achieve the sculpted effect. Do not apply highlights on top of shadows. This will cause a muddy makeup effect on the face that will look blotchy and unnatural.

To apply highlights and shadows with greasepaint sticks, apply directly or with a brush or toothpick. Blend into the foundation with

Types of Makeup

- Cake makeup comes in a wide range of colors. It is grease-less and should be applied with a sponge. It is fairly easy to apply and provides a smooth foundation.
- Creme makeup is velvety, nongreasy, and easy to remove. It should be applied with fingers or a brush. Powder must be applied over creme makeup to prevent shininess.
- Greasepaint is an inexpensive traditional foundation paint available in a wide range of colors, and it comes in stick, jar, or tube form. It is often used to achieve a specific skin tone and is good for covering blemishes. Powder must be applied on top of greasepaint. The stronger colors of stick-form greasepaint are called liners or shading colors, and they are useful for painting lines, highlights, lips, and shadows. One drawback to this foundation is that it rubs off easily on clothing.
- Makeup pencils are wooden pencils filled with greasepaint. They come in a variety of colors and are good for drawing lines and darkening eyebrows.
- Face powder is used to set the foundation. It is applied with a brush. One neutral transparent shade can be used on all cast members, as the powder should not distort the shade of foundation.
- Hair whitener comes in liquid or solid form. It is brushed or combed on, making hair look grey. To remove hair whitener, use soap and water.
- Makeup removers come in different forms. Cleansing cream is available at the drugstore. Greasepaint and creme makeup can be removed with liquid paraffin, cold cream, or baby oil. Cake makeup should be removed with soap and water.
- Spirit gum is an adhesive used to attach mustaches and beards, as well as the front lace of wigs.

the fingertips. Remember that this effect should be carefully blended. Done correctly, the audience should not be able to tell where highlighting and shadowing were used on the face.

The final step in makeup is the finishing touches. At this stage, eye shadow, eyeliner, mascara, and rouge (if necessary) are applied. Then, the face should be powdered one last time to keep everything in place.

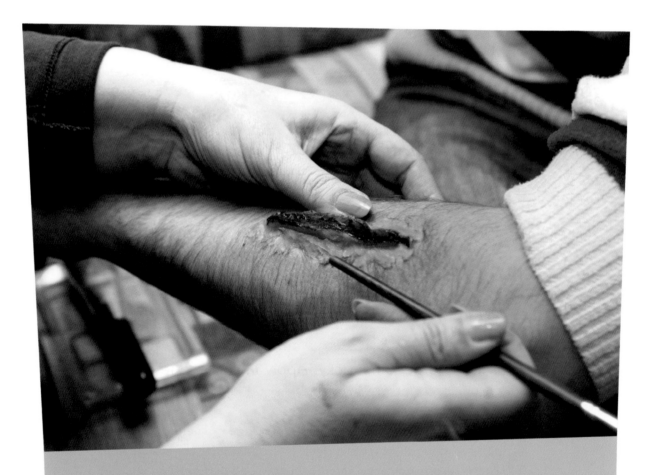

Creating a deep scar with makeup requires liquid latex and the patience to allow the liquid latex to dry properly. A bloody scar can be achieved by adding red paint.

How to Create a Deep Scar

A deep scar is created with liquid latex, which you can buy at any costume shop. Brush the latex onto the area where the scar will appear. Once the latex is dry, squeeze it together to form a crease. If the scar needs to look bloody, cover it with fake blood and wipe off the paint.

How to Give a Boy a Mustache or Beard

You can purchase self-adhesive fake beards and mustaches at any costume shop. If you don't have access to one, check hobby stores for synthetic hair used in doll making.

On the professional stage, in order to achieve certain shades of hair or specific effects, fake mustaches and beards are made from crepe hair. Crepe hair is sold in braided hanks and must be unwound and straightened before it can be used. To straighten it, the crepe hair is held over a steaming kettle. Two colors of hair can be mixed a few strands at a time to create a realistic effect.

Fake beards and mustaches that are not self-adhesive are attached to the face using spirit gum. Paint the area of the face where the mustache or beard should be attached with spirit gum and wait for it to become tacky. Apply the hairs a few at a time, using longer hairs than needed. When applying a beard, start at the base under the chin. Press the hair to the face using the flat blade of a pair of scissors or a damp towel. Work upward, applying the mustache last in two separate pieces. When all the hair is in place, trim the beard to the desired length and shape.

How to Age a Face Using Makeup

Aging a young face is a matter of understanding where muscles sag, revealing bones and the hollows of a face. Before starting the task of making a teenage face look older, collect photographs of old faces. Examine the face for shadowy areas. Highlighting these areas will look more realistic than simply drawing lines to indicate wrinkles.

Choose a foundation that is paler than the actor's skin tone. To

The right hair can help create a full look for a character. If the desired look cannot be achieved with the actor's own hair, try using a wig instead.

darken hollows in the face, mix a brick red with a grey shade and lightly dust on. Highlight the cheekbones and chin with a white powder to indicate a loss of fat in the face and use a little of the shadow to create a sunken look. Narrow the nose with the brick red and grey mixture, and use the white powder where needed. Age the mouth by turning down the corners and reducing the width of the lips. Finally, lighten the eyebrows and eyelashes with white powder.

Getting this look right may take a few tries, but done correctly, it will enhance a character's look and a high school actor's believability playing roles like Fagan in *Oliver!* and Edith Bouvier Beale in *Grey Gardens.*

Hair

For a high school production, it is best to use an actor's real hair. Wigs are expensive to rent, and the budget can be better used for costumes and accessories.

Each actor should bring in personal combs and brushes to be kept with the costumes during dress rehearsals and the run of the show. The head hairstylist will have pins, hair elastics, gel, mousse, hair spray, a spray bottle, hot rollers, a curling iron, hair tint, and a hair dryer on hand to assist with hairstyles. It is best to keep hair simple, unless the time period of the musical requires complicated and dramatic hair. If that is the case, be sure to do some research to keep your actors' hair historically accurate! Remember that an actor's eyes should not be covered by hair. If there are numerous dance numbers, consider creating looks that pull the hair away from the face.

Ready, Set, Go!

The week before the show is the time for last-minute adjustments and corrections to costumes, hair, and makeup. During technical and dress rehearsals, the creative team will be able to spot anything that needs improvement. The wardrobe supervisor and a team of volunteers should make repairs and last-minute alterations to the costumes, as well as develop a plan to clean and care for garments and accessories.

The Dressing Room

A week before the show opens, all the costumes should be ready. The wardrobe supervisor should check each item against a master list of costumes. Once it is confirmed that every costume is ready, it is time to set up the dressing room. During dress rehearsals and for the duration of the show's run, actors should complete all costume changes in a dressing room.

During the final dress rehearsal, actors wear full costumes, hair, and makeup. It is the last chance for the creative team to make any big changes—or minor adjustments—to a character's look.

The wardrobe supervisor is in charge of organizing a space for each actor. A list of costumes by scene should be taped next to each actor's wardrobe rack to avoid any confusion or oversight. The costume area for each actor should be organized carefully for quick costume changes. You might even want to create a system where each costume is kept on a hanger that is labeled with both the name of the actor and the name of the character. Though actors should be responsible for maintaining a tidy area, it is up to the wardrobe supervisor to ensure that everything is in place before the start of every dress rehearsal and show.

The Temporary Wardrobe

The wardrobe supervisor should set up a temporary maintenance wardrobe room near the stage and dressing area. The room should have a lockable door to prevent theft and tampering before the production opens. If possible, the temporary wardrobe should have a sink nearby with running hot and cold water. It also might be beneficial to find a space large enough for an ironing board and iron, emergency cleaning sprays, a large supply of coat hangers, and hanging racks for the costumes—perhaps even a sewing machine if space allows for it! The wardrobe supervisor should be in charge of taking pieces home for immediate laundering if a costume needs to be cleaned. No one involved with the production should remove costumes from the dressing area or temporary wardrobe except for the wardrobe supervisor! Actors must change out of costumes at the end of the night and leave everything in the dressing area.

Costume Care

There should be a plan for laundering and cleaning costumes, as stage makeup and dance numbers will cause stains and soiling of fabrics. Make a list of which costumes need to be dry-cleaned or hand washed, and which can be washed regularly. A schedule for laundry should be made according to the length of the run. Actors should be given T-shirts to wear under costumes to keep everything as clean and easy to launder as possible.

There should be a costume repair kit on hand for the dress rehearsals and the entire run of the show. The kit should contain needles, button thread, cottons, pins, safety pins, tapes, fastenings, buttons, scissors, seam ripper, latex adhesive, contact adhesive, a glue gun, extra fabric, extra trim, hemming tape, stick-on soles for footwear (to silence loud soles), and inner soles in case shoes are uncomfortable.

A cleaning kit is necessary for keeping costumes looking as fresh on closing night as on opening night. The kit should include detergent, soap flakes, dye remover, bleach, a stain-removal pen, fuller's earth (for grease removal), a clothes brush, a small scrubbing brush, shoe polish, and a shoe brush.

Dress Parade, Technical Rehearsal, Dress Rehearsal, and Final Rehearsal

A final fitting takes place before the dress rehearsal. This is called a dress parade. The director should be on hand at this fitting to see every costume. He or she can request any last-minute changes or point out any possible problems that may arise with specific garments. The costume designer, wardrobe supervisor, and any sewing volunteers must complete all changes within forty-eight hours so that actors can try on costumes one more time before the dress rehearsal.

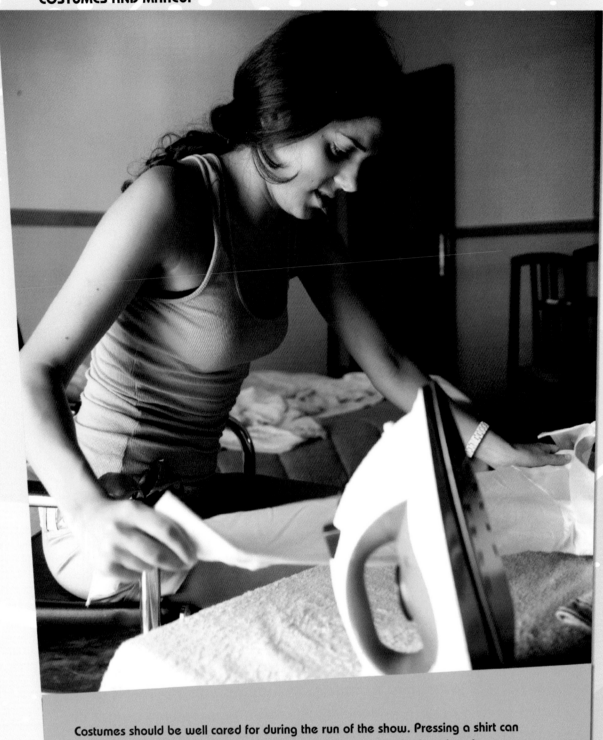

Costumes should be well cared for during the run of the show. Pressing a shirt can make it look cleaner and crisper, which is helpful if it cannot be laundered.

Full hair and makeup should be worn for the technical rehearsal. At this time, the makeup artist can see if the makeup looks natural under the stage lights and can make adjustments as needed. Some makeup that looked perfect under regular lights will not fare well under brighter spotlights. This is a normal occurrence; the makeup artist should not be frustrated when it happens. Understudies, if any, should also have hair and makeup tested under the lights at this time.

At the dress rehearsal, hair and makeup should be finalized. Another costume fitting can take place right after the dress rehearsal if any problems arise. This is the last opportunity to make any major costume changes. All alternations must be made that same evening so that the costume is ready for the next day's final rehearsal.

During the Run of the Show

During the run of the show, the wardrobe supervisor, costume designer, dressers, head makeup artist, and head hairstylist should be backstage at all times to help with costume changes and the retouching of hair and makeup. Plan on having the right number of helpers backstage. There should not be any extra people crowding the dressing areas, but there should be enough volunteers to ensure that everything runs smoothly. Some costume changes may occur in less than thirty seconds and actors will require help getting in and out of complicated dresses and suits. It is important that everyone knows his or her role backstage.

After the Show

On closing night, actors should claim the items they lent to the production. The wardrobe supervisor should keep track of which

As you can see, a single scene in a musical production requires careful attention to costumes, makeup, and hair. Without these three things, a production may come across as drab and dull.

items must be cleaned and returned and which items can be cleaned and stored at school. It is very important to return all items in good condition and in a timely fashion to ensure that productions in following years receive the same support from donors, rental agencies, teachers, and parents. The success of the production helps build a foundation for other musicals to be staged at school.

cake makeup A greaseless foundation that should be applied with a sponge; it does not require powder.

cold cream A type of makeup remover used in stage productions.

costumer designer Person in charge of the costumes for the show, from research to design to acquisition.

creative team The team of people—director, musical director, choreographer, and set, costume, lighting, and sound designers—who between them conceive and plan the entire production.

creme makeup A velvety, nongreasy type of foundation that should be applied with the fingers or a brush and covered with powder.

crepe hair Artificial hair used for creating mustaches and beards.

director The person in overall control of all artistic and creative elements of the show.

dress parade The final check of costumes by the director and costume designer before the dress rehearsal.

dress rehearsal Rehearsal in which performers dress in full costume and makeup.

face powder A type of makeup for keeping foundation in place and highlighting and shadowing the face.

foundation Base makeup used on the face.

greasepaint A type of foundation that comes in stick, jar, and tube form.

house Relating to the auditorium in which the musical is performed and the audience.

lead A principal actor, usually the largest or most important part in the show.

libretto The printed script of all dialogue and lyrics.

polyester wadding A lightweight and washable material used for padding costumes.

run Every performance from opening to closing night.

spirit gum A type of adhesive used to affix false facial hair.

tacking stitch A long, running stitch made by hand.

tailor's chalk A hard chalk used to make temporary markings on clothes.

thrift store A secondhand shop that often carries old clothing and accessories.

understudy Actor who studies another actor's part so that he or she can substitute in an emergency.

wardrobe supervisor Person in charge of the costumes once they have been acquired or made.

Broadway at the Center

Virginia Musical Theatre, Inc.
228 N. Lynnhaven Road, Suite 114
Virginia Beach, VA 23452
(757) 340.5446
E-mail: office@vmtheatre.org
Web site: http://www.broadwayatthecenter.com
Broadway at the Center is a leading musical theater company.

NYU Steinhardt Summer Program

Department of Music and Performing Arts
35 West 4th Street, Suite 777
New York, NY 10012
(212) 998-5424
Web site: http://steinhardt.nyu.edu/music/summer
New York University's Steinhardt Department of Music and Performing
    Arts Professions has a summer program for high school students.

Theatre Under the Stars

2099 Beach Avenue
Stanley Park
Vancouver, BC V6G 1Z4
Canada
(604) 734-1917
E-mail: info@tuts.ca
Web site: http://www.tuts.ca
This Canadian musical theater company stages productions for the
    summer months.

UCLA Arts Camp
UCLA School of Theater, Film, and Television
102 East Melnitz Hall
Los Angeles, CA 90095
(888) 497-3553
Web site: http://legacy.tft.ucla.edu/artscamp
UCLA Arts Camp is a summer musical theater conservatory for students
 ages sixteen to twenty-two.

University of Michigan School of Music, Theatre & Dance
E.V. Moore Building
1100 Baits Drive
Ann Arbor, MI 48109-2085
(734) 763-1279
E-mail: michyouthensembles@umich.edu
Web site: http://www.music.umich.edu/special_programs/youth
University of Michigan has summer youth programs in musical theater.

Web Sites

Due to the changing nature of Internet links, Rosen Publishing has developed an online list of Web sites related to the subject of this book. This site is updated regularly. Please use this link to access the list:

http://www.rosenlinks.com/hsm/cost

Davis, Gretchen, and Mindy Hall. *The Makeup Artist Handbook: Techniques for Film, Television, Photography, and Theatre*. Boston, MA: Focal Press, 2008.

Friedman, Lisa. *Break a Leg!: The Kid's Guide to Acting and Stagecraft*. New York, NY: Workman Publishing Company, 2002.

Kenrick, John. *Musical Theatre: A History*. Harrisburg, PA: Continuum International Publishing Group, 2008.

Lerch, Louise. *The Teen's Musical Theatre Collection: Young Woman's Collection*. Milwaukee, WI: Hal Leonard Corporation, 2001.

Miller, Scott. *Strike Up the Band: A New History of Musical Theatre*. Portsmouth, NH: Heinemann Drama, 2006.

Peterson, Lenka. *Kids Take the Stage: Helping Young People Discover the Creative Outlet of Theater*. New York, NY: Back Stage Books, 2006.

Corson, Richard, and James Glavan. *Stage Makeup*. Austin, TX: Allyn and Bacon, 2001.

Emerald, Jack. *Make-up in Amateur Movies, Drama, and Photography*. London, England: Fountain Press, 1966.

Gardyne, John. *Producing Musicals: A Practical Guide*. Ramsbury, England: The Crowood Press, Ltd., 2004.

Haynes, Elizabeth, and Theodore Cohen. *Make-up and Costume*. Edmonton, Canada: The Institute of Applied Art, Ltd., 1935.

Holt, Michael. *Costume and Make-up*. Oxford, England: Phaidon Press Limited, 1988.

Novak, Elaine A., and Deborah Novack. *Staging Musical Theatre: A Complete Guide for Directors, Choreographers and Producers*. Cincinnati, OH: Betterway Books, 1996.

Ratliff, Gerald Lee, and Suzanne Trauth. *On Stage: Producing Musical Theatre*. New York, NY: The Rosen Publishing Group, Inc., 1988.

Smith, C. Ray. *The Theatre Crafts Book of Make-up, Masks, and Wigs*. Emmaus, PA: Rodale Press, Inc., 1974.

Smith, Jerry. *The Chicago Tribune*. "Costume Maker and Performer." July 8, 2008. Retrieved July 23, 2008 (http://archives.chicagotribune.com/2008/jul/08/news/chi-hed-andersonjul08).

Tumbusch, Tom. *Complete Production Guide to Modern Musical Theatre*. New York, NY: Richards Rosen Press, Inc., 1969.

Wolters, N. E. B. *Modern Make-up for Stage and Screen*. London, England: Lovat Dickson Limited, 1937.

About the Author

Doretta Lau is an arts and culture writer living in Vancouver, Canada. She has acted in a number of high school productions.

Photo Credits

Cover (background), p. 1 Gaye Gerard/Getty Images; cover (inset) © Peter Hvizdak/The Image Works; pp. 4–5, 11 © Bob Daemmrich/The Image Works; pp. 8–9 © Jeff Greenberg/The Image Works; pp. 14–15 Stuart Wilson/Getty Images; p. 18 © www.istockphoto.com/Nancy Louie; pp. 21, 31, 38, 51 © ArenaPal/Topham/The Image Works; pp. 22–23 © www.istockphoto.com/Chris Schmidt; p. 25 © Mary Evans Picture Library/The Image Works; p. 27 © www.istockphoto.com/Cristian Lazzari; p. 33 Andrew H. Walker/Getty Images; p. 36 © Jim West/The Image Works; p. 41 China Photos/Getty Images; pp. 42–43 © Kayte M. Deioma/Photo Edit; p. 46 © www.istockphoto.com/Sergey Lavrentev; p. 48 Tim Sloan/AFP/Getty Images; p. 54 © www.istockphoto.com/Alija; p. 56 © Tony Freeman/Photo Edit.

Designer: Sam Zavieh; Editor: Bethany Bryan
Photo Researcher: Cindy Reiman